SUSHI & WINE
寿司とワイン

発　　　行	2017年4月1日
発 行 元	**有限会社 レーベン**
	〒105-0004
	東京都港区新橋1-8-4 丸忠ビル B1
	TEL.03(3573)0179　FAX.03(3573)0180
発 売 元	**株式会社 ガイアブックス**
	〒107-0052
	東京都港区赤坂1丁目1番地 細川ビル2F
	TEL.03(3585)2214　FAX.03(3585)1090
	http://www.gaiajapan.co.jp
印 刷 所	モリモト印刷株式会社

Copyright © 2017 Reben Co., Ltd.
ISBN978-4-88282-984-3 C0077

落丁本・乱丁本はお取り替えいたします。
本書を許可なく複製することは、かたくお断わりします。

著者：
江戸 西音 (えど　さいおん)
1949年東京生まれ。本名、星野和夫。
1972年千葉大学卒業。
1973年ベルリン工科大学留学後、フォトグラファーとして活動。
1980年帰国。著書に『ドイツワイン全書』(柴田書店)、ポケットブック『ドイツワイン』(鎌倉書房)、監修書に『FINE WINE シリーズドイツ』(ガイアブックス) など。
『世界の名酒辞典』(講談社) のドイツワインを担当。
2003年ドイツ連邦共和国より国家功労十字勲章受章。

絵・製作：
モキュート株式会社
http://mokyu-to.com/

寿司とワイン
― SUSHI & WINE ―

テキスト
江戸 西音
絵
モキュート

登場人物

最上 形造
最上寿司の次男でピアニスト。ベルリン音楽大学を卒業し帰国。某音楽大学でピアノ科の講師をしている。繊細な感覚の持ち主。

美山 まどか
形造のガールフレンド、フォトスタジオの受付をしている女の子。寿司が大好き。形造のピアノ演奏を聴いて恋してしまった。

阿部 呑
写真家、フォトスタジオのオーナー。グルメで美味しいものに目が無い。美山まどかの上司。さまざまな分野に造詣が深い。

最上 徳造
最上寿司の店主、形造の父。腕はいいが、昔ながらの寿司職人。寿司店も競合状態で、将来を少なからず案じている。

最上 修造
形造の兄、父親と一緒に最上寿司を営業している。真面目だが父親には頭が上がらない。いずれは後を継ぐつもりでいる。

野星 一夫
ドイツワイン専門店、銀座ワイナックス店主。寿司とワインの新しい形を発案、国内のみならず、ドイツでも寿司とワインの楽しみを広めている。

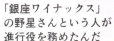

「銀座ワイナックス」の野星さんという人が進行役を務めたんだ

ふうん 何か特別なことがあったのか？

それがね うちが寿司屋だから寿司はよく知ってるけど

あれはびっくりしたよ

へぇー

ドイツにそんなすごい寿司があるのか

そうじゃないんだ

寿司の食べ方が特別なんだ

特別な…食べ方？

ドイツ優良ワイン生産者協会
VDP PRÄDIKATSWEINGÜTER

1910年創立、ドイツワイン生産のエリート団体。
ドイツ各生産地域に支部があり、現在２００有余の生産者が加盟。
葡萄の糖度だけではなくテロワールを重視した格付けを導入。
会員が生産するワインは、ボトルのカプセルに鷲のロゴマークが付いている。特に辛口ワインについては、最高級品をグローセス・ゲヴェクスと称し、シュペートレーゼ以上でも、Q.b.A と表示しているので注意が必要。

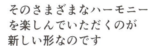

子持ち昆布

ニシンが昆布に産み付けた卵。天然物は稀で、産卵に押し寄せたニシンを昆布を垂らした生簀に追い込み人工的に産み付けさせる。カナダやアラスカからの輸入物が殆ど。

ゼクト（ドイツ産スパークリングワイン）

シャンパンという名称はフランスでもシャンパーニュ地方以外では使用できない。そのためドイツではシャンパンと同じ製法で生産したスパークリングワインに「ゼクト」(Sekt)という名称を使用している。リースリングゼクトやピノゼクト（主にピノ・ノワール）が多いが、シャルドネ、ムスカテラー、ジルヴァーナのものもある。シャンパンに比べ味わいもバラエティーに富んでいる。

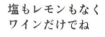

ヒラメ

淡泊美味、寿司には重要なネタ。左ヒラメに右カレイといい、目が体の左側に寄っている。西洋料理でも高級食材であり養殖ものも多い。冬物、寒ビラメは特に好まれる。

ヴァイスブルグンダー（ピノ・ブラン）

ドイツではピノ系品種の栽培が漸増傾向にあり、ピノ・ブランが世界一の生産量であることはほとんど知られていない。約５０００ヘクタールの栽培面積は全世界の３分の１を占める。産地や生産者により様々な特徴のワインが生産され、バリック、ノンバリック両方のタイプがあるが、特に和食にマッチするものは後者である。

でもゲーテは大のワイン好きだったんですね

彼は文学だけでなく自然科学の分野でも「色彩論」を書いたりしてるんだよね

僕も高校生のときゲーテの「若きヴェルテルの悩み」を読んだけど

ワインの話は出てこなかった気がするな

えーそれは知りませんでした

彼は科学者でもあったんですか！

ボタン海老

日本特産のエビ、１０月から５月に獲れ、ねっとりした甘い味わいは寿司ネタとして人気がある。最初は全てオスで、性転換して産卵するため、大きなものはメスばかりという。１１月から産卵前の３月頃までが旬である。

ジルヴァーナ

ジルヴァーナはドイツの伝統品種で３５０年前の栽培が確認されている。栽培面積はドイツ全体の５％ほどであるが、特にフランケンでは全体の２４％を占める重要品種である。リースリングが金ならジルヴァーナは銀といえる。酸は穏やかであるが上質のものは長期熟成ができる。

ホタテ

グルタミン酸やグリコーゲンを含み、心地よい歯応えと旨みがある。さまざまな料理に利用されるが、寿司にも人気のネタ。北海道、青森が主産地で養殖ものがほとんどである。一年中食べられるが、旬は冬で身が引き締まっておいしい。

ブラン・ド・ノワール

英語でいえば文字通りホワイト・オブ・ブラック、黒からの白ということになる。黒葡萄は赤ワインの原料だが、収穫後に破砕して果皮から色が出るのを待つ。圧搾後、果皮を除去してしまうと淡い白ワインのような搾汁が得られる。これを発酵させたものがブラン・ド・ノワールで、原料葡萄が通常の白ワイン用葡萄ではないので、独特の味わいがある。

うん、塩漬けした豚のすね肉をゆでた料理なんだ

これにはザウワークラウトという酢キャベツがついているんだ

マスタードをつけて食べる柔らかな豚肉はなんともいえない

酸のきいたリースリングが実によく合うんだ

おいしそうねそういうの

コハダの酢とリースリングの酸が合うのですがコハダは酢の味だけではありません

コハダ特有の深い味わいがありますので

ワインはカビネットよりボディのあるシュペートレーゼ級がおすすめです

このワインはクーベーアーですがグローセス・ゲヴェクスというシュペートレーゼ級のワインです

コハダ

光り物の中でも個性的な存在。シンコ、コハダ、ナカズミ、コノシロと成長するにつれて名前が変わる。下ごしらえが重要で職人の技がわかるネタ。味わいが強く、終わりに食すのが通で、寿司はコハダでとどめを刺すともいう。

リースリング

ドイツが誇る白ワインの重要品種。ドイツの全葡萄の中で最大の22％の作付けがある。モーゼルやラインガウのワインは古くから世界中に知られている。リースリングはその堅固な酸に特徴があり、シュペートレーゼ級で10～20年、アウスレーゼ級では30年以上貯蔵可能なものもある。辛口から極甘まで様々なワインが生産されており、貴腐ワインやアイスワインにおいてはリースリングに勝るものはない。ドイツは全世界のリースリング作付の70％を占めている。

皆様いかがでしたでしょうか　ここで前半の終了ということにして

少しPause(パウゼ)をはさんで後半に移りたいと思います

しばしご休憩を

前半だけでも実に興味深いけどまだ後半があるんだね

後半は何が出るのかな

寿司もワインと合わせると新しい味わいが生まれるんですね

私はもうかなり満腹気味だけど後半もがんばらなくちゃ

マグロの刺身

メジマグロやミナミマグロもあるが、何といってもホンマグロが王様である。赤身、中トロ、大トロなど部位別で寿司ネタになるが、これらをすべて楽しむには刺身が一番である。
赤身のヅケは適度な酸味と旨みが身にしみるし、中トロの心地よい食感と脂味、大トロの濃厚な甘みに近い味わいは比類がない。

リースリングワインの生産

ドイツには旧西ドイツに１１、旧東ドイツに２つの合計１３のワイン生産地がある。リースリングが栽培されていない産地はないが、その割合には大差がある。量的に多いのはプファルツやラインヘッセン、比率が高いのはモーゼルやラインガウである。後者にいたっては８０％近くをリースリングが占める。逆にフランケンでは数パーセントしかないのは意外であろう。

赤貝

赤い色はヘモグロビンを含むためで、プリプリした食感とエレガントな味わいは寿司ネタとしても貴重。北海道から九州まで分布するが、国内ものは少なくなり、中国や韓国からの輸入ものが多くなっている。12月から3月が旬である。

ロゼワインの種類

ドイツには幾つかのロゼワインがある。まず一般的なロゼ、これは黒葡萄を破砕した後、果皮から少し色が出た段階で搾汁をとり発酵させて作る。もう一つは、黒葡萄を破砕せずプレスし、ほとんど色がでていない搾汁を発酵させて作る淡い色のワイン。単一品種から作り、ヴァイスヘルプストと呼ばれる。またバーデンには、白ワイン用葡萄と赤ワイン用黒葡萄を混ぜてプレス、発酵させて作るロートリングもある（白ワインと赤ワインをブレンドするものではない）。

ゲヴュルツトラミナーは
あん肝にも合いまして

この場合は
先ほどお話しした
バーデン産の
シュペートレーゼ
がいいのですが

またの機会に
いたしましょう

まあ
残念だわ

まったくだね
で、今度は何が
出てくるのかな

ウニ

北海道の利尻、礼文のバフンウニ、長崎のアカウニなど寿司にはたまらない高級ネタがある。黄色の微細な粒の塊は未成熟のオスの精巣やメスの卵巣で、ビタミン B1、B2 や EPA 等を含んでいる。寿司屋では通年提供されているが、旬は産地により異なり、一般には 6 月から 9 月ごろまでと言われている。

ゲヴュルツトラミナー

ドイツの葡萄栽培総面積の 1% にも満たないが、これほど個性的な品種はないだろう。ゲヴュルツは英語のスパイスのことで、その名のとおりスパイシーな味わい、野ばらのような香り、心地よい色とコクが魅力である。フランスのアルザス産に比べドイツ産は、産地により生産者によりバラエティー豊かである。特に、フォアグラやレバーまたウニなどに美味しい。

生産者は
フランツ・ケラーで
シュペートブルグンダー
セレクションAです

セレクションという名称は
ドイツワイン基金が
2000年から高級辛口ワイン
のカテゴリーとして
導入したものです

すでにこの名称を使用
していた生産者は

2010年まで継続使用
が認められています

なおAは
アウスレーゼ級を
意味するもので

アウスレーゼと
いわないのは
甘いワインと
間違われないため
と思われます

なるほどね
赤ワインが
甘いと思われちゃ
困るよね

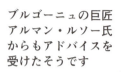

VDPグローセス・ゲヴェクス＝最高級辛口系ドイツワイン

ドイツのワイン法は葡萄の糖度を基準にしており、クーベーアー、カビネット、シュペートレーゼ・・・と必要糖度が高くなるので、カビネットよりシュペートレーゼの方が甘く、アウスレーゼは更に甘いと思われがちである。しかしシュペートレーゼでも辛口は多くあり（ラベルにトロッケン＝trockenの表示がある）アウスレーゼでさえも辛口は存在する。VDPは消費者に明示するため、最上級の畑＝グローセ・ラーゲから生産される辛口系ワインだけをグローセス・ゲヴェクス（優秀生産物）と呼び、ロゴ付き指定ボトルを使用するか、メインラベルに略称GGを、またカプセルにVDP GROSSE LAGEと表示するなどを推奨している。

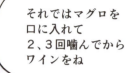

大トロの炙り

マグロの腹の下部、脂が最も多い部分で、江戸時代は赤身だけを食し捨てられていたという。現在は最も高級な部位として珍重されている。海外でも赤身を食し、トロの部分は日本の寿司が知られてから、食すようになった。炙ると香ばしく、また旨みが深まるので、生のものとは一味も二味も違う楽しみが生まれる。

シュペートブルグンダー（ピノ・ノワール）

１９９０年代になってからドイツの赤ワイン生産は急速に進み、特にシュペートブルグンダー（ピノ・ノワール）は全葡萄栽培面積の１１.５％を占めるに至り、フランス、アメリカに次いで世界第３位となった。バーデン、プファルツ、アールの生産地には世界的なレベルの赤ワイン生産者が現れている。フランス産に比べ、コストパフォーマンスが高く、ピノ・ノワールの愛好者は要注目である。

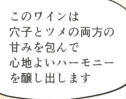
このワインは穴子とツメの両方の甘みを包んで心地よいハーモニーを醸し出します

なるほどね
ちょうどいい残糖のワインがあるのもすごい

本当にドイツワインの多様さには驚きだ
でもそれを入手できないのが残念だね

そうですね
奥が深いのにその一部しか味わえないのはもったいない

穴子

ウナギによく似た魚で多くの種類がある。海底で半身だけを海中に出している姿からこの名がついたらしい。日本で食されるのは浅い海に生息するマアナゴで、江戸時代から東京湾の羽田沖で獲れたものが本場ものとされてきた。ふっくらした口の中でとけるような肉質は人気があり、寿司ではツメと呼ぶ煮詰めたタレをまぶして食すが、天ぷらにも好まれる食材である。

シュペートレーゼ

シュペートは遅い、レーゼは摘み取りの意味で、遅摘みのワインを指す。ドイツでは初摘み、遅摘みと収穫時期により別々のワインにするのが普通である。収穫を遅らすことで葡萄の糖度が高まり、飲みごたえのあるワインができる。各生産地ごと、また葡萄の品種ごとにシュペートレーゼとして認定される必要糖度が定められている。より下の等級への格下げ表示は可能なので、甘い印象を避けるため、あえて Q.ｂ.A. 表示をする辛口ワインもある。

タマゴ

寿司屋のタマゴは、家庭の卵焼きとは違う。それは食べた瞬間に気が付くであろう。店のこだわりが現れる大切なネタである。醤油、みりん、だし汁などの他に山芋、芝エビ、白身魚をすり潰したものなどを卵に加えたり、その店により工夫があり、じっくり時間をかけて焼く。いつ食べるかはお客の自由だが、最後のデザートとしても楽しめる。

アイスワイン

アイスワイン（ドイツではアイスヴァイン）は収穫を12月、場合によっては翌年1月まで遅らせ、気温がマイナス7度以下になって氷結状態になった葡萄から作る。葡萄内の水分だけが果皮外に氷って析出する結果、濃縮した搾汁が得られ、濃厚で甘いワインができる。一般的に貴腐ワインより酸が多いさっぱりした甘味が特徴で、数十年は寝かせることができる。温暖化が進み収穫できる年は少なくなっている。

あとがき

もうかなり昔の１９７０年代、ベルリンに在住していた頃、ドイツワインを飲み始めた。当時は白ワインが多かったが、その多様性、また和食によく合うことに驚かされた。

ドイツワインといえばリースリングだとよく言われる。確かにリースリングはドイツが誇る最重要品種である。だが、その栽培面積は全体の２２％に過ぎず、他の様々な品種にもすばらしいワインがある。

ドイツでは、小規模生産者でも２０〜３０種類ものワインを生産している。多くの品種をブレンドせず別々に、また同一品種でも早摘みと遅摘みを別々に仕上げるからである。
いろいろな品種の極辛から極甘まで、実に様々なワインが存在し、誰もが好みのワインを見つけることができる。
このような多様性故に、寿司ネタの一貫一貫に合うワインを見出すことも可能なのである。本書は実話をもとに、ドイツワインの知られざる魅力を理解して頂くのに最適と考え、マンガの形で刊行いたしました。

そんなすばらしい会なら一度体験したいという皆様は、銀座ワイナックスへ是非お問い合わせ下さい。銀座ワイナックスは実在します。

刊行にあたり、モキュート株式会社 ならびに 株式会社ガイアブックスご両社のご協力に心から謝意を表します。

江戸 西音

Postscript

In the 1970s, I stayed in Berlin and started to drink German wine; it feels like ages ago now. At the time, white wines were all the rage, and I remember being surprised at the variety available and at how well they went with Japanese food.

Many people think German wine equals Riesling. And while it's true that Riesling is an important and pride-worthy variety to the Germans, it only makes up 22% of the country's total planted area, and there are many other wonderful wines being produced there.

In Germany, even small scale wineries produce 20 to 30 kinds of wine. This is because they make wines from many different grape varieties and also make different wines from a single variety by harvesting the grapes at different times. As a result, everyone is able to find a wine that suits their tastes as there is such a wide selection to choose from. You can find both dry and sweet wines of many varieties.

It is because of this diversity that it's possible to find a wine that pairs well with each individual sushi topping. Based on a true story, we decided to publish this book as a manga because we determined it as the best and most interesting way to introduce the little-known appeal of German wines.

If this book left you wanting to experience sushi and wine for yourself, please contact Ginza Winax, which exists in the real world as well.

I deeply thank both mokyu-to, Inc. and Gaia Books Inc. for their support and for helping make this publication possible. Thank you.

Saion Edo

To be continued.

They go especially well with Japanese cuisine.

Let's give a round of applause to tonight's sushi chefs and service staff!

clap clap clap clap

Sweet egg custard wrapped in dried seaweed (Tamago)

Eggs in a sushi restaurant aren't your everyday fried eggs. This should become apparent right after your first bite. "Tamago," as it's called, is one of the most representative sushi toppings of any restaurant. Usually made with soy sauce, sweet sake, and soup stock, sometimes yam, shiba shrimp, or minced white fish are added to the eggs. Each restaurant has its own special way of making tamago. It can be eaten at any point during the meal, sometimes even as dessert!

Eiswein

Eiswein, or "ice wine" in English, is wine made from naturally frozen grapes. Harvest requires temperatures of at least minus 7 °C, and in Germany, this often ends up being in late December or the following January. Since the water in the grapes freezes on the outside of their skins, you can make very sweet wine from the concentrated juices left inside. Eiswein contains high acidity levels, so it's more refreshing than Trockenbeerenauslese, and it can be stored for several decades. However, the production of Eiswein is becoming more and more difficult due to global warming.

Conger eel (Anago)

There are many kinds of conger eel, which are very similar to eel. Since they inhabit only shallow parts of the sea, they're called "anago," meaning ana-no-ko (hole dwellers), in Japanese. The anago caught near Haneda in Tokyo Bay have had a reputation of being the best since the Edo period. Famous for its plump and melty texture, conger eel sushi is usually brushed with a boiled down sauce called "tsume." It's also commonly eaten as tempura.

Spätlese

Wine made from late-harvested grapes. "Spät" means "late," and "lese" means "harvest." In Germany, different wines are made from late-harvested grapes and early-harvested grapes. Naturally, late-harvested grapes contain more sugar than early-harvested ones, and they yield wines with a rich body. The standards of Spätlese (sugar content) vary by both region and grape variety. And since it is possible to downgrade wines to a lower quality grade, dry Spätlese level wines will often be labeled as QbA to avoid confusing them for a sweet wine.

Broiled fatty tuna (Otoro no aburi)

Fatty tuna comes from the lower part of the tuna's belly, which is the most fatty part. It is said that during the Edo period, only lean tuna was eaten and the fatty portions discarded. Today, it is prized as being the most valuable part of the fish. Lean tuna has always commonly been eaten overseas, but the popularity of fatty tuna has been on the rise since the introduction of sushi. And while it's delicious enough raw, broiling tuna really enhances its flavor and is another way to enjoy it.

Spätburgunder (Pinot Noir)

Red wine production in Germany began to develop rapidly in the 1990s. The Pinot Noir variety now accounts for 11.5% of Germany's total planted area. And they are now the third largest producer in the world, after France and the USA. Many winemakers in the regions of Baden, Württemberg, Pfalz, Ahr, etc. produce excellent wines of the highest quality, yet price-wise they are much more affordable for Pinot lovers compared with French products.

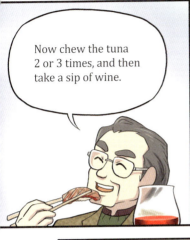

The current vineyard owner, Fritz Keller, apparently received advice from Burgundy's legendary Armand Rousseau when he was young.

Germany sure has some interesting wine producers.

VDP Grosses Gewächs
=The highest grade of dry German wines

German wine laws are based on the sugar content of picked grapes. The more sugar the higher the level. Because of this, many consumers tend to think a Spätlese is sweeter than a Kabinett, and an Auslese even more so. However, there are many dry and semi-dry Spätlese, which are labeled as "trocken" and "halbtrocken." You can even find dry Auslese wines sometimes. So the VDP introduced a new category, Grosses Gewächs, which denotes top-quality dry wines from designated Grosse Lage vineyards. These wines come in special bottles with a logo or GG mark indication on the label. It is also recommended that "VDP GROSSE LAGE" appear on the wines' capsules.

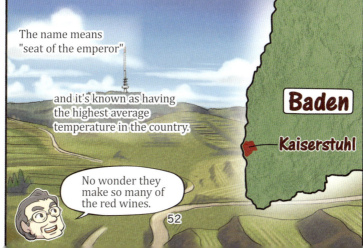

Sea urchin roe (Uni)

The ezobafun-uni from Rishiri, Hokkaido and the red sea urchin from Nagasaki are among the most high-grade sushi toppings out there. Though referred to as the roe (eggs), uni is actually the premature animal's gonads (which produce the roe), and the only edible portion of it. They are a rich source of vitamin B1, B2, EPA, and more. Sea urchins are usually in season from June until September, but it varies by area of origin.

Gewürztraminer

While this grape only accounts for less than 1% of Germany's total vines, its wine is aromatic and unique in taste, with hints of wild rose on the nose, a lovely color, and a full body. "Gewürz" means "spice" in German. Gewürztraminer wines from Germany vary greatly according to region and winery compared with wines from other regions. They pair well with foie gras, liver, sea urchin, etc.

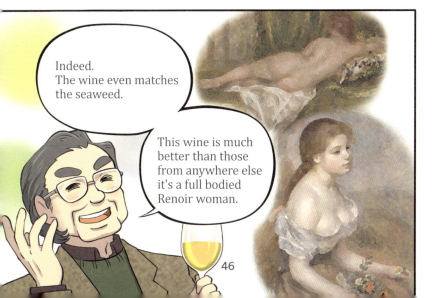

The wine-making region of Württemberg is located around Stuttgart.

Because 70% of the wine produced there is red wine, you can be sure that they have some real gems.

I would've never guessed there were areas producing so much red wine.

I love red wine. I've been waiting for it to make an appearance tonight.

Ark shell (Akagai)

Their red color, which is caused by hemoglobin, is rather striking, but it's their fresh texture and elegant taste that makes them a favorite of many. While ark shells are distributed all over Japan, most often they are imported from China or Korea, not domestic. Ark shells are best enjoyed when in season from December to March.

Rosé wine in Germany

Rosé wine is made from red wine grapes. Usually, the juice is left in contact with the skins just long enough for it to change color slightly; it's then fermented further to raise the alcohol content. Another type of rosé is Weissherbst, which is also made with red wine grapes, but is pressed without any contact time. As a result, its color is much lighter than the former. There's also Rotling from Baden, a rosé made by blending red and white wine grapes together before pressing.

"I hope everyone is enjoying themselves thus far. As the first half of the event is about to draw to a close, let's take a few moments and enjoy a short break before recommencing."

"The event has been interesting enough already, and it's only halfway done!"

"I can't wait to find out what's next."

"I didn't know so many new flavors could be created by combining sushi and wine."

"I'm starting to get pretty full, but I don't want to miss out on the second half!"

Tuna sashimi (Maguro no sashimi)

There are many types of tuna, including young tuna and southern bluefin tuna, but the Pacific bluefin tuna remains the king of all tuna. Although several different parts of the fish are used as sushi toppings, such as fatty tuna, medium fatty tuna, and lean tuna, the best way to enjoy it is as sashimi. Zuke has moderate acidity and umami, medium fatty tuna has a pleasant chewy texture and tasty amount of fat, and fatty tuna's rich flavor is simply unparalleled.

Production of Riesling wine

There are 13 wine making regions in Germany: 11 in former West Germany and 2 in former East Germany. Riesling is produced more or less in each of these regions. However, the ratio of Riesling to other varieties varies greatly. Pfalz and Rheinhessen are the production leaders, but Mosel and Rheingau both have high ratios of up to 80% as well. On the other side of things, Riesling doesn't even make up 5% of Franken's production.

He eventually ended up marrying her.

This family has links to Japan as well.

Important Cultural Properties/Former Shuzo Aoki House

Shuzo Aoki, a diplomat during the Meiji period, had a granddaughter named Hissa who married into the Neipperg family.

Oh, wow. A bottle of wine with a story that stretches across the globe. How fascinating!

Who'd have thought that Japan had a link to German nobility!

Gizzard shad (Kohada)

A very unique silver-skinned fish with a name that changes as it matures. First they're called shinko, then kohada, then nakazumi, and finally konoshiro. Preparation is extremely important, so ordering this fish is a good way to gauge a sushi chef's skills. Since its flavor is powerful, it's generally saved for last. There's even a saying, "a meal of sushi should end with gizzard shad."

Riesling

As the most famous German white wine grape, it makes up 22% of the country's total planted area. Mosel and Rheingau have enjoyed an excellent reputation for their Riesling for many years. With their robust acidity, Spätlese level wines can be enjoyed for 10~20 years and Auslese level wines for often over 30 years. Everything from dry to noble sweet wines are produced. And you won't find a better variety for Trockenbeerenauslese and Eiswein. Germany produces 70% of the world's Riesling.

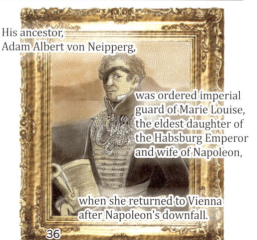

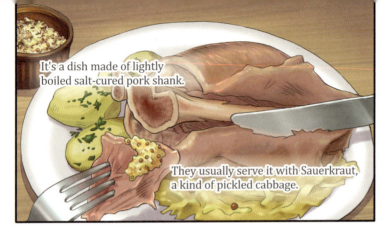

Riesling is popular for its unique acidity which is referred to as "Schöne Säure," meaning "wonderful acid."

However, the acidity of dry wines is too strong for most Japanese food, with tempura etc. being the exception.

But since gizzard shad is marinated in vinegar, you'll find it pairs with Riesling quite well.

I suppose this wine's acidity *is* rather prominent,

but it sure tastes great with the gizzard shad. I'm impressed.

When I was in Germany, this is what we used to drink

when eating Eisbein with pickled cabbage.

What's Eisbein?

Gently broiling scallops really enhances their flavor,

and pairing them with a Spätlese level Grauburgunder, which is a Pinot Gris, is another way of doing so.

That's very interesting.

Let's ask my brother to try this next time.

Sounds like a plan!

Scallop (Hotate)

Scallops contain glutamic acid and glycogen, and they have a pleasant chewy texture and excellent umami flavor. They are used in various dishes and are also widely enjoyed as a sushi topping. Main production areas are Hokkaido and Aomori, where most of them are farmed. And while they're available year round, their meat becomes delectably firmer in the winter season.

Blanc de Noir

Literally "white of black." Blanc de Noir is a white wine made from red wine grapes. After being pressed, even black grapes produce a light colored juice. It is the pigment in the skins that makes red wine red, so by removing the skins before fermentation, white wine can be produced. As this wine uses red wine grapes, it has a unique taste, which differs greatly from other white wines.

I know I read Goethe's *The Sorrows of Young Werther* when I was in high school,

but I don't remember there being much mention of wine.

So he was a wine lover, huh?

Goethe didn't just write literature though, he also wrote about chromatics in the field of natural science.

I didn't know he was a scientist, too!

Botan shrimp (Botan ebi)

This is a Japanese specialty shrimp that can be caught from October to May. It's popular as a sushi topping due to its sweet taste and sticky texture. Botan shrimp are always born male, but change sex when spawning, so the bigger botan shrimp are all female.

Silvaner

Silvaner is a traditional German grape which is known for its 350-year cultivation history. This grape accounts for 5% of Germany's total cultivation, but in the Franken region it accounts for 24%. If Riesling were gold, Silvaner would be silver. Though its acidity is gentle, it is known to age quite well.

This wine is one of the area's Kabinett, a feinherb.

Feinherb is a newer word that can be literally translated as meaning "exquisite dry," though in regular terms it would be called an off-dry.

They also produce halbtrocken, which is a half-dry wine.

Mmmm. This is a little sweeter than the last one.

Since botan shrimp are already sweet, it makes sense that a wine containing residual sugar was selected.

Ah, I see. Well, they sure do have nice harmony.

And the acidity isn't as noticeable as the Riesling's.

What's next? I'm so excited!

I wonder if we're allowed to eat the pickled ginger...

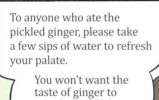

To anyone who ate the pickled ginger, please take a few sips of water to refresh your palate.

You won't want the taste of ginger to interfere with the next pairing.

The next combination is botan shrimp and Silvaner.

Silvaner has a long history in Germany, just like Riesling.

The Franken area around Würzburg, which is the starting point of the Romantic Road, is particularly famous for it.

Flounder (Hirame)

Light and delicious, this is a very important sushi topping. There is a saying in Japan, "left-eye flounder (hirame), right-eye flounder (karei)." The eyes of a flounder (hirame) are on the left side of its body. Considered a luxury food in the west as well, a large percentage come from fish farms. Kan-birame is preferred in the winter season.

Weissburgunder (Pinot Blanc)

Production of the Pinot family of grapes is increasing little by little in Germany. Few people know, however, that Germany produces the most Pinot Blanc in the world. There are 5,000 ha of Pinot Blanc in Germany, about 1/3 of the world's total planted area. A great variety of wines are made with these grapes in many different regions, both barrique and non-barrique; the latter of which go wonderfully with Japanese cuisine.

Herring roe on kelp (Komochi konbu)

Herring roe deposited on kombu, a type of kelp. Finding it in nature is quite rare, so it's usually farmed by putting herring about to spawn in an enclosure filled with kelp. It's mainly imported from Canada and Alaska.

Sekt (German Sparkling wine)

The name "Champagne" can only be used for sparkling wine produced in the Champagne region of France. In Germany, they use the name "Sekt" for sparkling wine made by the Champagne method. Riesling and Pinot Noir grapes are a popular choice, but you can also find Sekt made from Chardonnay, Muskateller, and Silvaner. Compared to Champagne, Sekt offers flavor variety.

but Mr. Noboshi of Ginza Winax was running the show.

Hmm

Was it anything special?

I know quite a lot about sushi, as it is the family business,

but this event surprised even me!

Was the sushi in Germany really that good?

Actually, it was the *way* they ate it that was extraordinary.

Extraordinary?

VDP PRÄDIKATSWEINGÜTER

An association of elite German wine producers. Founded in 1910, it is made up of about 200 members in many wine producing regions. Its classification of wine is based especially on terroir (a region's climate, soils, and terrain). VDP wine bottles have a capsule with an eagle logo. Top quality dry wines are called "Grosses Gewächs," and are classified as QbA even if they are Spätlese level or higher.

Characters

Keizo Mogami
Pianist and second son of Mogami Sushi. Returned to Japan after graduating from Berlin Music University. Teaches piano at a certain music university. Is a man of refined taste.

Madoka Miyama
Girlfriend of Keizo and photo studio receptionist. Loves sushi. Fell in love with Keizo after hearing him play the piano.

Don Abe
Photographer and owner of a photo studio. An avid foodie, partial to delicious food. Boss of Madoka Miyama. Knowledgeable about many subjects.

Tokuzo Mogami
Owner of Mogami Sushi and Keizo's father. Highly skilled but old-fashioned sushi chef. Running a competitive sushi restaurant, he worries about its future.

Shuzo Mogami
Older brother of Keizo. Runs Mogami Sushi with his father. Diligent but no match for his father. Willing to carry on the family business.

Kazuo Noboshi
Owner of Ginza Winax, a German wine specialty shop. Mastermind behind "The New Way to Enjoy Sushi and Wine." Dedicated to spreading the enjoyment of sushi and wine not only around Japan, but also Germany.

SUSHI & WINE

The New Way to Enjoy Sushi and Wine

Text
Saion Edo

Picture
mokyu-to

Copyright © 2017 Reben Co., Ltd.
ISBN978-4-88282-984-3 C0077